COMO Shambhala Estate, Bali, Indonesia

深い森の中のコテージに泊まる。コモ・シャンバラ・エステートでは、そんなエキゾティックな宿泊体験ができる。
You will feel as if you stay at a cottage in deep forest at COMO Shambhala Estate.

「シワ消える！コモ・シャンバラ」の秘密の一つがこの聖なる泉だ。
One of the secrets that "we come wrinkle-free at COMO Shambhala" is this sacred spring.

本書のタイトルは「シワ消える！コモ・シャンバラ」だが、最初にその種明かしをしたい。実は、コモ・シャンバラ・エステートのハイドロ・セラピーを受けると、私の経験では、一時的（数日間程度）ではあるが、シワが劇的に減り、肌がプルンとするのだ。

　ハイドロ・セラピーはヴァイタリティ・プールと呼ばれる特殊なプールで行われる。そのプールの水がポイントだ。リゾート敷地内から湧き出る聖なる泉（左写真）の水を、ドイツ製のナノ水にする機械を使い、浸透圧の強いミネラル豊富なナノ水にする。その水のプールに浸かることでシワが消えるという寸法だ。

　やってみて気付いたが、「水遁の術」でも使わない限り（あるいは、シュノーケルの器具を使わない限り）顔を水につけ続けることは難しい。ただ、努力して、水を顔にヒタヒタとつけるだけでも効果があった。お見苦しくて恐縮だが、その効果が次のページ以降の「使用前」「使用後」の写真だ。

　First, I would like to tell you how you can come "wrinkle-free" as in the title of this book. Your skin comes virtually wrinkle-free by taking "Hydrotherapy" at "Vitality Pool" at COMO Shambhara Estate. The secret is in the special water that fills the pool. It is "nano-water" made from their mineral rich spring water of the sacred spring located in the property. Composition of this spring water is broken into very fine particles by a German machine. The osmotic pressure of nano-water is so strong that you can see distinctive change in my face (not a very good model) in the following pages.

1

インドネシアのデンパサール空港から車で60-90分。ウブドの町を通過し、最後は車の通れない細い橋を歩いて渡る。荷物は運んでもらえる。

About 60 to 90 minutes by car from Denpasar-Bali airport, Indonesia. At the last step, we cross a narrow bridge on foot to the resort.

2

泊まった部屋はEstate Suite。独立した建物で、斜面に突き出て立っているのでプライバシーはばっちり。

The room I stayed at was Estate Suite, an indepedent house built on the edge of the slope. So it has strict privacy.

3

鉱水がわき出る「聖なる泉」の源泉は、急斜面を約10分下ったところにある。行きはよいよい、帰りは急斜面の上りで、大変だ。

The source of the "Sacred Spring" is located at the place 10 minutes down on the steep slope. The way back is so tough.

4

これが、その聖なる水をナノ水にしたVaitality Poolだ。椅子がたくさんあるがそれぞれ泡が吹き出る位置が違う。数分おきに椅子を移動する。

This is the Vitality Pool with the nano-water from the sacred spring. At each chair in the pool, bubble stream comes differently.

5 BEFORE

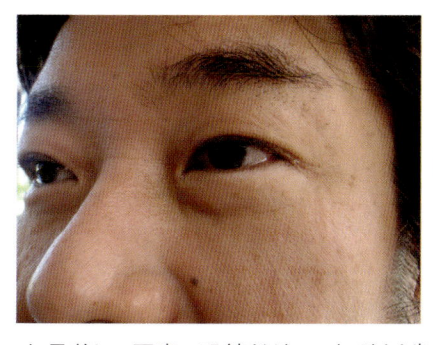

お見苦しい写真で恐縮だが、これが44歳の普通の肌だ。それなりにシワ、シミ、弛みがある。これがプールに入る前の写真だ。

I am so sorry to show you this non-beautiful photo. This is me, 44 years old with wrinkles and spots. This photo is before I took the Pool.

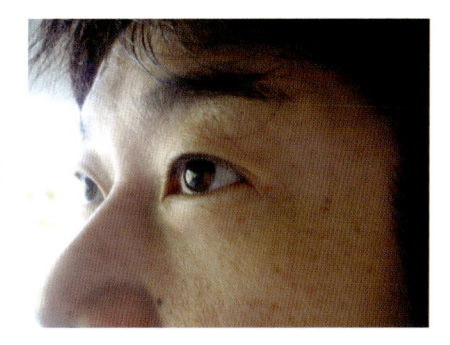

6 AFTER

これがプールの後の写真だ。明らかにシワが減っている。数歳は若く見える。顔全体も引き締まってみえるのは気のせいだろうか。

This is the photo after I took the Pool. It looks obviously that wrinkles were reduced a lot. I looked yonger by a couple of years.

7

コモ・シャンバラ・エステートは食事もおいしい。朝食は、世界中どこも同じような食事が出そうな気もするだろうが、ここはバリならではの朝食だ。

Food served here is delicious. We can taste the Balinese breakfast here, though you may think breakfast is same anywahere.

8

フルーツサラダ。日本の高級果物屋には様々なフルーツがあるので、珍しいものはないが、敷地内でとれたフルーツだからフレッシュで美味。

"Fruits Salad", each fruit of wihich is not uncommon, but they are fresh and good, as this estate yields these fruits.

9

夕食のメニューにはミエゴレン（インドネシア風焼きそば）もある。値段は18万とあり驚くが、だいたい100ルピア＝1円だ（09年11月現在）。

We can take Mie Goreng, Indonesian fried noodles. The price was 180,000, but roughly saying US$1 is Indonesia Rupiah 10,000.

10

デザートのアボカドのタルト。クリーム状にした生のアボカドに蜂蜜を掛けたもの。生の食材には豊富な酵素が含まれるという考えに基づいた食事だ。

Avocado tart as desert. It is raw avocado paste with honey. It is based on the idea that raw materials include a lot of enzyme.

11

コモ・シャンバラ・エステートではパーソナル・アシスタントがつく。彼の名はアガス。礼儀正しく、よく気のきく賢い青年だ。滞在が一層快適になる。

Each room has each personal asistant. His name is Agus, always polite and smart. He made my stay much more comfortable.

リゾート名： 　コモ・シャンバラ・エステート
Resort Name： 　COMO Shambhala Estate
場所(Place)：インドネシアのバリ（Bali, Indonesia）
　　URL：／／www.cse.como.bz
　　TEL：＋62-361-978-888
料金　ガーデンルーム　　　US＄300〜
　　　エステート・スイート　US＄650〜
　　　※朝食付。税・サービス料で21％加算。
Price　Garden Room　　US＄300〜
　　　Estate Suite　US＄650〜
　　　※ breakfast. included.
　　　 Addtional +21%, service charge and tax,

壁に魚が泳ぐ。
シンガポールの新しい滞在先、カペラ・シンガポール
Many fishes swim on the wall.
A new destination in Singapore is here.

Capella Singapore

シンガポールのチャンギ空港は巨大だ。空港を出るだけで疲れる。JetQuayのエスコートサービスを利用すると、飛行機を降りたところに迎えがきていて、カートで移動。ラウンジでくつろぐ間に、預け荷物も回収してくれる。

JetQuay provides an escort service at Changi airport, Singapore. Prior booking is good.

www.jetquay.com.sg

カペラ・シンガポールは、2009年3月末にシンガポールのセントーサ島にできた新しいリゾートホテルだ。古い植民地時代の建物に、現代的な建物を組み合わせた独特のデザインだ。

Capella Singapore is a new resort at Sentosa Island, Singapore, opened in March, 2009. It looks unique as it is a combination between a colonial building and a modern designed one.

室内もスタイリッシュだ。これはベッドサイドのコントロールパネルだが、これを触るだけでカーテンの開け閉めも含め、すべてを操作できる。僕にはモダンすぎるが。
It is stylish inside rooms, too. This photo shows the control panel at bedside. Touching it controls everything including blinds. It is too modern for me though.

さきほど紹介したコモ・シャンバラ（〜P6）があるバリ・デンパサール空港へは、成田からの直行便にファーストクラスの設定がない（09年11月現在）。シンガポールまでファーストクラスで移動し、1泊してからバリに行く方がくつろげる。

I recommend you to go to Singapore by First Class seat from Tokyo, as the direct flight from Tokyo to Bali does not have First Class, when you go to COMO Shambhala Estate introduced before(-P6).

メインダイニングのCASSIAは、モダン・チャイニーズ。ここも洗練された空間だ。
The main dining here is "CASSIA", a modern chinese place, very stylish, too.

リゾート名：　　　カペラ・シンガポール
Resort Name：　　Capella Singapore
場所(Place)：シンガポール (Singapore)
URL：//capellasingapore.com
TEL：+65-6377-8888
料金　デラックス・ルーム　S＄750〜
　　　セントーサ・スイート　S＄1,000
　　　※朝食なし。税7%・サービス料10%加算。
Price　Delux Room S＄750〜
　　　Sentosa Suite　S＄1,000
　　　※ Without Breakfast.
　　　　Addtional 10%service charge and 7% tax,
※　S＄1（シンガポール・ドル）＝JPY65（約65円）
（2009年11月時点）

Six Senses Hideaway
Zighy Bay, Oman

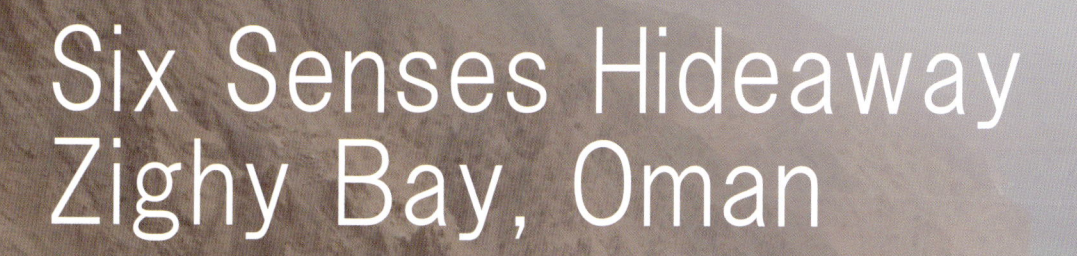

パラグライダーでチェックイン！　と聞いて、血が騒ぐのは
私だけだろうか？　行き先は右側の遥か彼方遠くのホテルだ。
Checking-in by paraglider! Is it only me,, who gets excited to hear that?
The destination in this photo is the place in the right side, very far away.

12

このリゾートは岩山で囲まれた湾に建てられている。山を越えない限り、陸路ではアクセスすることができない。
　「パラグライダーでチェックイン」と言っても、当然ながら希望者だけ。強制ではない。また、インストラクターが後ろについている。私も生まれて初めてのパラグライダーだったが、何の支障もなかった。
　パラグライダーを希望しない人は、四輪駆動車で岩山の道なき道をクネクネと下りていく。四輪駆動車での移動もスリル満点だ。崖すれすれを通っていく。、「えっ、こんなにギリギリ？　落ちないの？」とひやひやするが、ドライバーは慣れていて平然とした顔で運転する。
　聞いたところでは、パラグライダーでチェックインする人の方が圧倒的に少数派のようだ。
　このリゾートの良さはエキゾティックなところだ。左の写真のように、建物はあえて、現地の素材を使い、昔ながらの建物のように作ってある。もちろん設備は最新のものだ。食事も中東料理が多く、中東を満喫できる

　It is not mandatory to check in by paraglider. Those who do not want to do that go there by four-wheel drive car, which is also thrilling. You may feel that the car might fall off the edge of the cliff, but don't be concerned, your driver is very skilled.
Ground transportation is far more popular than by air, although it is quite safe, with an instructor flies with you rignt behind you. Six Senses Hideaway Zighy Bay is very exotic. Each building is built with local materials, resembling traditional construction, but of course is equipped with the latest technology. You can enjoy teste of the Middle East, too.

13

1 オマーンにはマスカット空港があるが、このリゾートの最寄りは隣国のドバイ空港。一時期よりもさびれた感じだ。

The nearst airport to the resort is Dubai Airport, not an airport in Oman. Dubai airport looked less shiny because of the late crisis.

2 到着ラウンジで中東の「お約束」、歓迎のデーツ（ナツメヤシ）とアラビック・コーヒー。昔の名残のミネラル補給だ。

At the arrival lounge, dates and arabic coffee are served as established custom. They gave tourists in desert the minerals in the old age.

3 出迎えの四輪駆動車で、ドバイご自慢の6車線道路を走る。陸路でオマーンに入国。空港から約90分で到着する。

90 minitues drive by the four-wheel drive car takes you to the resort. We drive through six-lane expressway in Dubai and enter into Oman.

4 岩山の野生のヤギを見るようになると、リゾートは近い。リゾート敷地のゲートをくぐり、岩山を頂上まで車は登る。

Near the gate of the resort territory, we find wild goats in the rock mountain. The car go up to the peak of it.

5 頂上で待っているとインストラクターが来て、パラグライダーでのチェックイン準備が始まる。

The instructor came up to the peak and started the preparation to check in by paraglider together.

6 心の準備をする暇はない。インストラクターからの注意も一言だけ。「跳ぶな、座るな、ただ走れ」だ。

There was no time to prepare myself. The instructor told me "No jump, no sit. Just run" only.

7 曇り空で強風。私の心配をよそに彼は「今だ。走れ」とつぶやいた。私は転びそうになりながら走りだし空に浮いた。

Cloudy and very windy. Though I was nervous, he whispered to me "Now. Run." I started running and found myself in the air.

8 最短なら5分の距離を、約30分をかけてホテル脇の海岸に着陸だ。最後はジェットコースター並みのGがかかる。

30 minutes flight with going back and forth took me to the seashore next to the resort. On landing, I felt strong gravity like jet coaster.

15

エキゾティックな内装
The inside of the rooms is also exotic.

各部屋の庭にサマーハウスと呼ばれる伝統的な夕涼みスペースがある。

Each room has, what is called, "summer house" in each garden.

9 チェックイン後、最初にスパにあるハマムでの垢すりをお勧めする。長旅の汗とパラグライダーの冷や汗を流す。

After checking-in, I recommend you to go the SPA to take Hammam, a sauma in Middle East, with body scrub. You can refresh yourself.

10 SIX SENSES SPA では隣国ドバイの基礎化粧品を使う。世界的ブランドのアメニティには飽きているから、新鮮だ。

At SIX SENSES SPA, skin care products from Dubai, the next country, are used. The local brand was new for me.

11 敷地内には、デーツ（ナツメヤシ）の実が、たわわになっている。一見すると、変わったブドウのようだ。

You will find many date palm trees with plenty of fruits, inside the area of the resort. The fruit looks like a funny grape.

12 部屋の引き出しを開けると、メッカの方向を示す木が打ちつけられていた。QIBLA（一般的には KIBLA）と呼ぶ。

In opening a drawer in the room, I found a wooden round plate fixed, which shows the direction of Mecca, called generally "Kibla".

13 部屋によっては、お風呂が銅でぴかぴかだ。たまにはこういうバスタブに入るのも悪くない。

Some rooms have shiny bathtub made from Copper. It is not bad to take this kind of bath sometimes.

14 食事は中東の料理が多く美味だが、どういうわけか寿司もある。名前は「日本食の一研究」。回転ずしよりは美味。

We can enjoy Middle-Eastern food there, but I found Sushi somehow. The name of the dish is "A study in Japanese". The taste was OK.

15 パラグライダーで飛び降りる崖の上にレストラン Sense of The Edge がある。絶景だ。週末のみの営業。要予約だ。

At the cliff where I flied by paraglider, there is a restaurant named "Senses of The Edge." Open only on weekends. Reservation required.

16 ここでは各部屋にバトラー（執事）がつく。彼は香港出身のブライアン。ドランクドラゴンの鈴木そっくりのナイスガイ。

Each room has its butler. The gentleman in the photo was my bultler, Brian, from Hong Kong. He looks like a famous Japanese comedian.

リゾート名： シックス・センシズ・ハイダウェイ・ジギーベイ
Resort Name： Six Senses Hideaway, Zighy Bay
場所(Place)： オマーン（Oman）
URL：//www.sixsenses.com
TEL：+968-26735-555

料金　プールビラ　US＄900～

　　　プールビラスイート　US＄1200～

　　　※朝食なし。税9%・サービス料8.4%加算。

　　　※パラグライダーでのチェックインは別途US＄180＋Tax（17.4%）（一人当たり）

Price　Pool Villa　US＄900～

　　　Pool Villa Suite　US＄1200～

　　　※ Without Breakfast. Addtional 8.4% service charge and 9% tax

　　　※ Checking-in by Paraglider US$180 +Tax(17.4%) per person

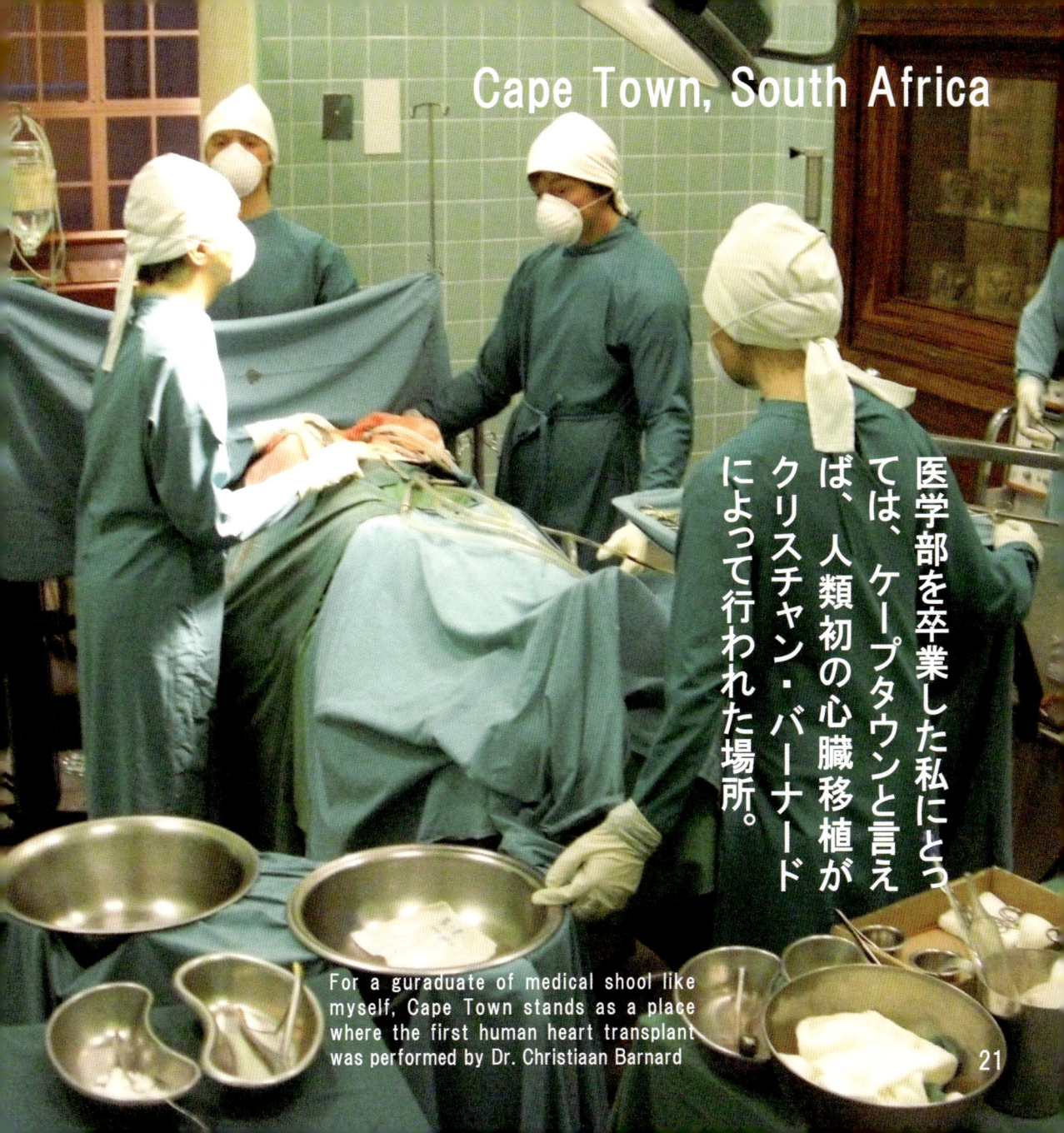

Cape Town, South Africa

医学部を卒業した私にとっては、ケープタウンと言えば、人類初の心臓移植がクリスチャン・バーナードによって行われた場所。

For a guraduate of medical shool like myself, Cape Town stands as a place where the first human heart transplant was performed by Dr. Christiaan Barnard

21

1　前頁の写真は、手術現場の蝋人形での展示だ。元グルート・スキュール病院が今は博物館になっている。

The photo on the previous page is wax figures display of the operation at "Heart of Cape Town Museum", ex-Groote Schuur Hospital.

2　人間の心臓移植がアメリカでなくなぜ南アか疑問に思うだろう。ハート・オブ・ケープタウン博物館には学者間の競争の様子や新聞等の展示がある。

You may think why the first human heart transplant was done in South Africa, not in U.S.. You may find out why from the materials there.

3　特殊な興味を除けば、ケープタウンと言えばテーブルマウンテンだろう。山にかかる雲は「テーブルクロス」と言う。

Generally Speaking, Cape Town is famous for Table Mountain. The cloud on Table Mountain is called "Tablecloth".

4　自分の足で登る人もいるが危険なのでケーブルウェイをお勧めする。香港のビクトリアピーク並みの急な傾斜に驚く。

I recommend you to take the cable way, rather than to climb. The cable way is so steep as the cable car at Victoria Peak in Hong Kong.

22

One&Only
Cape Town

今やケープタウンは、このリゾートに行くためだめに訪問してもよいくらいだ。世界一快適なリゾートとして。

To stay at this world's most comfortable resort has become the reason why to visit Cape Town; the One&Only Cape Town.

One&Onlyと聞くとゴージャスなオーシャン・リゾートをイメージするだろうが、ケープタウンは違う。派手よりはシック。ゴージャスよりも快適さ。見えないところにお金をかけ、快適さを追求している。南アは世界のどこから行っても遠い。疲れ果てて到着した身体をしっかり休める最高のベッド。大きな部屋と大きなバスタブ。スイッチ操作も直感的にできる、ほどよい近代化。動線を考えたタオルの置き方など、細かいところまで計算されつくされている。

One&Only resorts are famous for being gorgeous. But One&Only Cape Town is different. It is chic and comfortable, rather than gorgeous. They spend money not only for the surface, but also for the basic materials to make everything comfortable as much as possible.
South Africa is very far from anywhere in the world. we come very tired when we reach there.
One&Only Cape Towon provides a large and comfortable room, bed, and bathtub to let us relax. We can flick the switches intuitively there, though we have to do trial and error in the too modern hotels to find the proper switch. The position of towels looks to be considered well, supposing the typical movement line of the guests.

5 アメニティは現地南アのCharlotte Rhysを採用。もちろんオーガニックだが、フェア・トレードも考慮したものだ。

Charlotte Rhys, the local company, provides the skin care amernity. The materials are not only organic and but also purchaced by fair trade.

6 大きなバスタブでゆっくりと長旅の疲れを癒す。お湯の出方も豊富で気持ちがいい。

We can relax in the large bathtub in the room, after a long trip to Cape Town. We can enjoy the good volume of hot water from the tap.

7 1階にはNOBUがある。アフリカ大陸初のお店。ご存じの通り和食とは違うが、ナイスガイの日本人シェフがいる。

The resort has NOBU, a famous Japanese restaurant, which is the first place in the African Continent. A Japanese chef manages it.

8 ゴードン・ラムゼイのメイズというレストランも1階にある。南アの様々なおいしいワインのテイスティングが楽しめる。

This resort has "Maze" by Gordon Ramsay, too. We can enjoy many kinds of South African wine by tasting size.

25

「メイズ」は、ゴードン・ランゼイのアフリカ大陸初上陸の店。個人的にはロンドンのゴードン・ラムゼイ以上においしい気がした。素材のおいしさが生かされ、豊富な南アワインと一緒に楽しめる最高の食事を堪能してほしい。写真はPhillip Carmichaelヘッドシェフ。

"Maze" is also the first restaurant of Gordon Ramsey in the Africa Continent. I personally thought that the dishes of Maze were better than those of the restaurant in London. We can enjoy the taste of the good food materials with many kinds of South African wine. I think one of the best restaurants in the world. This picure is Mr. Philip Carmichael, the head chef.

9 客室のあるメインの建物とは別に、スパの島がある。

Apart from the main building of guest rooms, Spa is located in an island of the water garden.

10 サウナのそばに巨大かき氷マシーン（アイス・ファウンテン）がある。食べるためではなく（笑）、身体を冷やすためだ。

Near the sauna in the SPA area, we can make our body cool down by putting the shaved ice from the machine, called "ice fountain."

11 ホテルから徒歩5分。ショッピングモールがある。治安が不安な南アでも、ここでは昼間は一人で歩ける。

There is a large shopping mall from the resort by 5 minutes walk. Here you can walk by yourself in day time without anxiety of security.

12 ショッピングモールには大きなスーパーマーケットもある。南アワインも豊富な品ぞろえ。

The shopping mall has a large super market with many variety of the South African wines.

27

客室から眺めるテーブルマウンテンは圧巻だ。
The view of Table Mountain from the guest room is great.

リゾート名： ワン＆オンリー・ケープタウン
Resort Name： One&Only Cape Town

場所 (Place)： 南アフリカ共和国 ケープタウン （Cape Town, South Africa）

URL：//www.oneandonlycapetown.com

TEL：+27-21-431-5888

料金 マリーナ・ルーム ZAR（南ア・ランド） 6000〜
1ベッドルーム・アイランド・スイート ZAR13000〜

※朝食なし。消費税込。 旅行税1%別

※ 1 ZAR（南アフリカ・ランド）＝ 約12円（2010年1月現在）

Price： Marina Room ZAR (South Africa Rand) 6050〜
1Bedroom Island Suite ZAR13000〜

※ Without Breakfast. VAT included. 1% Tourism levy addtional.

※ 1 ZAR South Africa Rand）= US$ 0.13 （As of 2010 JAN）

Hospitality Ticket
FIFA World Cup

ここで紹介する「スイート・ホスピタリティ」の他に、会場傍での飲食ができる「ビジネス・シート」(US$950～)や「マッチパビリオン」(US$550～)もある。

Apart from "Suite Hospitality" introduced here, you can choose "Business Seat" (US$950～), where you can enjoy a meal at the near place to the stadium, or "Match Pavillion" (US$550～).

写真は2009年6月に南アフリカのヨハネスブルグで行われたFIFAコンフェデレーションズ・カップ決勝戦前のセレモニー。

This photo is the ceremony before the final game of FIFA Confederations Cup held in June, 2009 at Johanesburg, South Africa.

29

北海道育ちの私にとって、人ごみほど苦手なものはない。並ぶのもダメだ。だから女子から「ディズニーランドに連れてって！」などと言われると急に気分がブルーになる。スポーツ観戦もそういう意味で微妙だ。2009年3月にロスにWBCの決勝戦を観に行ったときも、ゲームは素晴らしかったが、行きの交通渋滞、球場内の混雑には辟易した。混雑回避を目指して、販売しているチケットで一番高いチケットを買ったが、それでも今一つだった。

　そういう私が「サッカーのワールドカップを観ることができるだろうか」と懸念していたところ、知人から、「ワールドカップにはホスピタリティーチケットというのがある。それはスタジアムへの出入り口も一般の観客とは別で、車も優先的に入れる。のんびりと食事をし、お酒を飲みながらゆったりと観戦できるよ。」と言われ、「本当かな？」と疑いを持ちながら2009年6月に、南アのワールドカップ1年前に開催されるコンフェデレーションズ・カップ（コンフェデ杯）の決勝戦を、ヨハネスブルグまで観に行った。コンフェデ杯では、ワールドカップ本番ほど値段は高くないが（一人500米ドル）ホスピタリティーチケットがあった。

1 スタジアムへの道路は3mおきに警官が並び安全だ。この特別なパスがあれば入口そばまで車が入ることができる。

It was safe, as policemen stood each 3 meters along the road to the studiam. My car entered ito the gate with the above special pass.

2 ホスピタリティ・チケットは高価なため、偽造防止の工夫もされている。ワールドカップ本番では一人最低950ドル。

This is the Hospitality Ticet. It has divices to avoid counterfeit, as the it is so expensive. The price starts from US$950 at FIFA World Cup.

3 専用ゲートを入ると、SUITEという表示がある。自分の部屋を目指す。

I found a sign of "SUITE", after I entered into the special gate of the studiam. I went to my SUITE room, looking at the sign.

4 ブッフェ方式の食事とフリードリンクで、観戦しながら食事ができる。外にでると通常の観覧席が用意されている。

I watched the game with enjoying buffet style foods and drinks. Outside of the SUITE room, there was normal seat area reserved.

Crowded places and waiting in long lines are two tihngs that I most detest, because I was born and raised in Hokkaido, a north countryside of Japan. The place is almost empty. I would suddenly be in a mood if someone askes me to take her to 'Tokyo Disneyland', because it is the place with long lines. I could not enjoy the final game of WBC baseball at Los Angeles on March 2009. It was a heavy traffic to go to the Dogers Stadium and the inside was also crowded, though the most expensive seat avaialble.

I wonder if I could enjoy FIFA World Cup games in 2010. My friend told me that "They have a special ticket called "Hospitality Ticket". The entrance to the stadiam is different from the others. You can enjoy watching the game with food and drinks in a comfortable room." So I went to experience the special seat of the final game of Confederations Cup held in June 2009 at Johanesburg. The price was US$500 a person.

5 SUITEの外の観客席は寒い。6月の南アは初冬だ。ダウンを着て、保温座布団、カイロ着用での観戦でちょうどよい。

It was cold outside of the SUITE in June at Johanesburg, winter time. I recomend you to wear a down jacket and put a seat cushion.

商品名： スイート・ホスピタリティ
Name of Ticket : Suite Hospitality
価格例：FIFA ワールドカップ 2010年6月24日の
　　　　日本 対 デンマーク 戦
　　　　一人 1,500 米ドル（最低 2 席の購入）
Price exapmle : Japan vs Denmark
　　　　　　　　on 24 JUN 2010, FIFA World Cup
　　　　　　　　US＄ 1,500 per person
　　　　　　　　（Mininum 2 people）
問合せ： 近畿日本ツーリスト（03-3255-7831）
　　　　　knt-sports@or.knt.co.jp
Contact : http:// hospitality. fifa. com

　南アフリカと言うと、「治安は大丈夫か？」と訊かれることもあるが、サッカー観戦に関してだけ言えば、危険な目には合わないだろう。同じ南アでも、ヨハネスブルグはケープタウンと違って緊張するが、それでもホテルからスタジアムへの道路は警官があふれ、信号で車が止まっても問題ない。現実的な問題は防寒対策だ。日本の冬のサッカー観戦の準備が必要だ。2010年は世界的な不景気が継続しているから、2010年2月現在でチケットがまだ残っている。来年以降景気が回復するとこの手のチケットはあっという間に売り切れる。

　いわゆるホスピタリティ・チケットは、新しいスポーツ観戦の方法として選択肢の一つにいれるべきだろう。

　I am sometimes asked "is South Africa safe?". I think it should be no problem in terms of going to the stadiam and watching the game. Main roads to the stadiam will be well protected by the police. There should be no danger, even when your car stops at signals. You should consider the protection against the cold weather, rather than safety.

　The hospitality tickets are still avaialble as of Feb 2010, because of the world wide recession. A "Hopspitality tikect" is a new alternative to enjoy the sport games.

Singita
Sabi Sand
South Africa

シンギタで野生動物を快適な環境で堪能する。
We enjoy watching wild animals in very comfortable surroundings at Singita Sabi Sand, South Africa.

シンギタでは運がいいと、いわゆるビッグファイブに会える。ビックファイブとは、ライオン、ヒョウ、サイ、象、ブァッファローのことだ。
At Singita, you may come across "Big Five", lion, leopard, rhino, elephant, and buffalo.

1 シンギタへは、ヨハネスブルグで Federal Air のセスナに乗り換える。乗り換え場所はわかりずらいので要注意。

We fly from Johannesburg International Airport with Federal Air in a Cessna. It is not very easy to find the way to Federal Air.

2 約1時間のフライト。飛行機の予約はホテルでやってくれる。料金は別料金で事前に請求される。

The flight takes about 1 hour and the booking was made by the resort. The fare is added to the your bill that is pre-paid.

3 朝夕、1日2回サファリに行く。それ以外にやることは特にない。4日間いれば合計8回参加する人がほとんどだ。

Almost everybody goes on safari in the early morning and late afternoon, twice a day. If you stay for 4 days, that's 8 safaris!

4 道路は草木がなく歩きやすいので、動物も道路を移動する。なので、路上でよく遭遇する。

It is easy for the animals to walk on the road as there are no trees and bushes. We see lots of animals on the road.

5 朝も夜も途中でおやつタイムがある。写真はガイドのコールマン。話題豊富で気が訊く優秀なガイドだ。

During the safari, both in the morning and afternoon, we stop for sun downer drinks and snacks. The Field Guide in the photo is Coleman.

6 サファリを一緒に回るので、他の宿泊客とも仲良くなれる。世界中からお金持ちと友達になれる。

You can make lots of friends on safari at Singita, people from all over the world.

7 野生のライオンもランドクルーザーのすぐそばを通るが、車に乗っている限り安全だ。

Wild lions came near our Land Rover. Although the vehicle is open, we are safe as long as we stay inside.

8 念のため、ランドクルーザーにはライフル銃が備え付けてある。

Just in case, the Land Rover has a rifle to protect us.

9 シンギタは食事もおいしく、部屋も近代的な設備で快適だ。レストランは屋外で川向うには動物も見える。

The restaurant at Singita serves delicious food. While you eat, you can look out for wild animals. The guest rooms are also comfortable.

10 料理ではアフリカのサバンナならではの料理がある。これはブレスボックというインパラ似の動物の腰肉だ。

I enjoyed trying the local meat from the African savannah. The photo is "Blesbok loin". Blesbok is an antelope.

客室の入口。アフリカの現地の素材とデザインでエキゾティックだ。
This is the entrance to the Suite It is exotic as the materials and designs are very African.

アフリカ風のインテリアだが、客室内の設備は非常に近代的。
The equipment in the Site is very modern, though the interior looks African.

リゾート名： シンギタ・サビ・サンド・ボールダーズロッジ
Resort Name： Singita Sabi Sand, Boulders Lodge
場所(Place)： 南アフリカ共和国 北東部 サビ砂漠 (Sabi Sand Private Game Reserve)
URL：//www.singita.com
TEL：+27-21-683-3424
料金： ラグジャリースイート ZAR（南ア・ランド）21900〜（2人1部屋の場合の一部屋一泊料金）
　　　※3食付。1日2回のサファリ含む。シャンパンを除くワインなど飲料代も含む。
　　　シンギタ空港送迎含む。消費税・旅行税込。

　　　※ 1 ZAR（南アフリカ・ランド）= 約12円（2010年1月現在）

Price： Luxury Suite ZAR South Africa Rand) 21900〜 per suite night
　　　※breakfast/lunch/dinner included. All drinks including wines included(champagne is not include)
　　　Two safaris a day included. Surface transfer from Singita airstrip to the lodges included.
　　　VAT & Tourism levy included.

　　　※ 1 ZAR South Africa Rand) = US$ 0.13 （As of 2010 Jan）

※ヨハネスブルグ・シンギタ間のFederal Airの料金は片道 約ZAR 2650
　　Federal Air Johannesburg to Singita (One way) ZAR 2691
　　Federal Air Singita to Johannesburg (One way) ZAR 2650

LA MAMOUNIA
Marrakech, Morocco

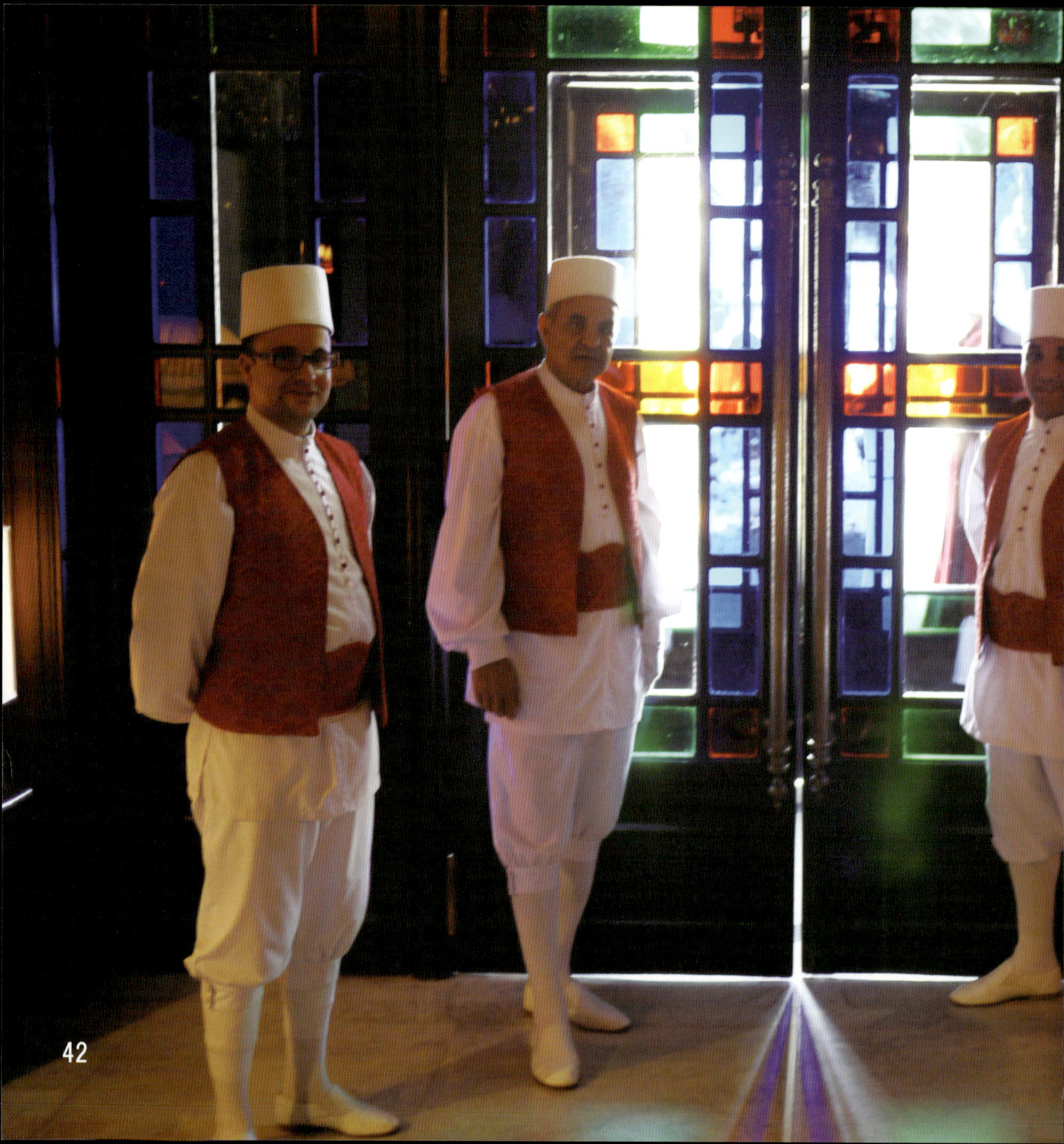

夜、遅いチェックインだった。建物に入った瞬間、思わずため息をついた。暗闇に美しく輝く色とりどりのステンドグラス。計算されつくした美しさ。ロビーのソファーに座ると、デーツとアーモンドミルクが差し出される。

　ため息の予感は、空港に迎えに来た最新型ジャガーに座った瞬間からあった。空港からホテルまで約10分。車の中は良い香りに満ち、座席前のスクリーンにはオリジナルの音楽と共にイメージDVDが映される。コンセプトがディテールにいたるまで徹底されている。それが嫌味でなく、男性でも夢見心地になってしまうほどだ。09年秋にリニューアル・オープンした「ラ・マモーニア」は世界で一番美しいホテルだろう。美しさを紙面で伝えきれないもどかしさを感じる。

　I checked in late at night. The moment I entered into the structure, I sighed in spite of myself. Stained-glass shining colorfully in the darkness. It was a beauty. Dates and almond milk were served, when I sat on the sofa at the lobby. Hunch of sigh began the moment I took a seat in the latest model of Jaguar, picking me up at the Marakesh airport. Perfume was filled in the car. DVD of the resort is played in the screen of the front seat back, with the original music. The concept of La Mamounia is completed even in the fine details. La Mamounia is the most beautiful resort all over the world. It is frusttating that the beauty is not fully describable in writing.

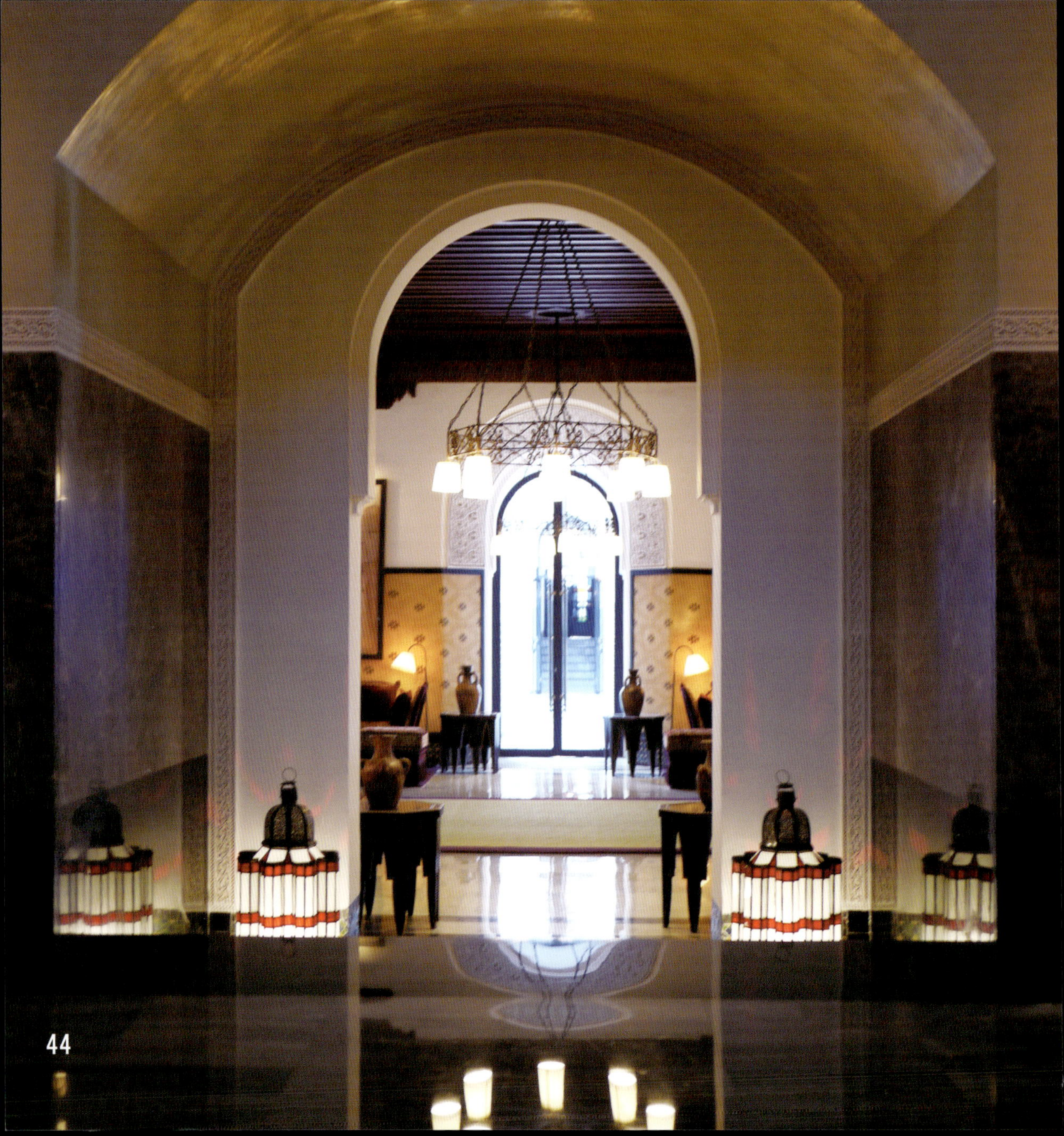

1 チャーチル・スイート。1930年代からラ・マモーニアは、ドゴールやチャップリンなど世界の著名人が宿泊してきた。

This photo is Churchill Suite. Many distinguished people, like Charles de Gaulle, Charlie Chaplin, have stayed at La Mamounia from 1930's.

2 朝食はテラスでモロッコの赤いバラを観ながら食べる。日差しは強いが、12月の朝は肌寒かった。

You have breakfast at the Terrace, looking at Moroccan red roses. The sunlight was strong, but it was a bit cold in early morning in Dec.

3 城壁で囲まれた庭園は赤や白のバラだけでなく様々な花が咲き乱れ美しく、静かだ。散歩するだけで心が落ち着く。

The garden surrounded by a high wall has not only red and white roses, but also many flowers. It is very quiet. We can enjoy walking.

4 ホテル内は美術館のように様々なオブジェがある。シャンデリアも見事だが、日差しも計算された配置だ。

The resort has lots of art works like an art museum. The chandelier is also great with consideration of sun light from the windows.

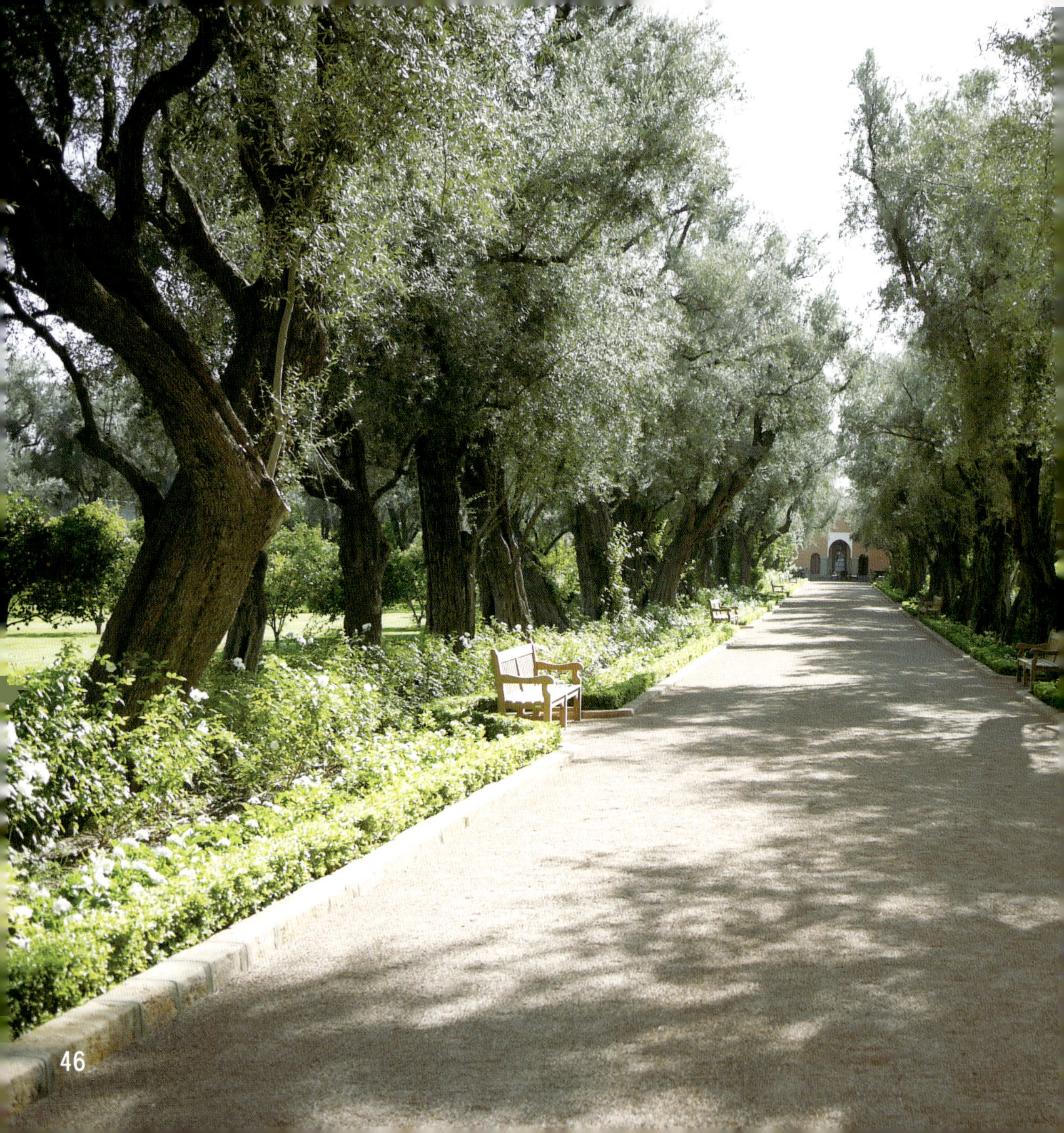

写真を見て不思議に思うことはあるだろうか。
　実は、左側のオリーブ並木に比べ、右側のオリーブ並木は道路ぎりぎりになっている。
　リオープンするにあたって、ホテルの窓から庭園の通路を見たときに、通路がまっすぐになるように右側に30センチほどずらしたという。そのぐらいラ・マモーニアの景色は計算されつくしている。
　庭園の奥では、レストランで提供する野菜を有機栽培している畑がある。
　この庭園の散歩は究極の散歩だと思う。小鳥がさえずり、美しい花々に囲まれ、まさにのどかで平和なひとときだ。

　Can you find anything funny in the photo in the left?
　If you look at it very carefully, you find that the right side olive trees' line is just near the road, compared to the left side trees' line.
　La Mamounia, when it was re-opened in 2009 Autumn, moved the road to right side by about 30 cm, in order for the guests to enjoy the perspective straightly from the window of the lobby area.
　This is a good example how deeply the views are designed with precise calculation.
　If you go into the depths of the garden, there is a field of organic vegetables, served in the restaurants there.
　The stroll in the garden gives you a peaceful time in the beautiful flowers.

マラケシュのシンボル・クトゥビヤモスク。ホテルから徒歩数分。スークの近くだ。
Al-Kutubiya, the symbol of Marrakech. Just a couple of minutes walk from the resort, located near the Souq.

5 ジャマ・エル・フナ広場（通称、フナ広場）。ホテルから徒歩5分。スークに隣接する。昼間は閑散としている。

Djemma El-Fna Square, 5 minutes walk from the resort. The Square is next to the Souq. It looks deserted in the daytime.....

6 夜8時を過ぎると、どこから湧き出てきたかわからないほどの人ごみに。多くの飲食のテントが登場。大道芸人も。

After 8 PM, the Square comes crowded. Lots of stands serving foods and drinks. Also many street performers show their performance.

7 フナ広場に隣接したスークはまるで迷路のようだ。カラフルな皮スリッパ「バブーシュ」等お土産には事欠かない。

The Souq, next to El-Fna Square, is a labyrinth. It has lots of souvenir shops, selling "Babouche", mules made from leather e.t.c.

8 「ファティマの手」は魔よけの土産。「グローバルプライス」や「デモクラティック・プライス」が登場すると値切りも潮時だ。

In negotiating the price of souvenirs, when the shop man says "global price" or "democratic price", it is a sign of the final stage.

49

モロッコ名物、モロカン・サラダ。ラ・マモーニアにあるレ・モロカンも美味。
The Moroccan Salad, the specialty in Morocco, at Le Moroccan in La Mamounia.

9 モロッコのお菓子。スーパーマーケットで購入したものを盛り付けた。スーパーはホテルからタクシーで20分ほど。

The Moroccan petit four, purchased at a super market, 20 minutes by taxi from the resort.

10 私は機会があれば、地元のビールやワインを賞味するように心がけている。写真はモロッコのビール「カサブランカ」。味は日本のビールより軽いが美味。

I try to taste local beers in anywhere. This is a Moroccan beer "Casablanca", which has lighter taste than Japanese beers.

11 ホテルでの食事も申し分ないが、せっかくなので、メディナ（旧市街）にある伝統的なレストラン・ヤクートにぜひ。

The food in the resort is great, but it is good to go to "Yacout", an traditional Moroccan restaurant, in Medina, the old town.

12 ヤクートのモロカン・サラダも美味。食べきれないほど出てくるが、食べきるものではないらしい。

The Moroccan Salad of Yacout is also tasty. The volume is too much to complete eating it. But you take what you eat from each dish.

ヤクートのチキンのタジン。ヤクートはメディナ（旧市街）の看板もない石作りの建物にある。薄暗い建物の中、暖炉の炎やロウソクがきらめく。奏でられる民族音楽。最高にロマンティックな雰囲気だ。

The photo is "Chcken Tajine". The restaurant "Yacout" is located at Medina, the old town, without any sign outside. In the dark building, a flame of the fireplace and lots of candles are shining. The local music is played. The most romantic atmosphere.

マラケシュほど、異国情緒にあふれる街はないだろう。
　これ以上ない喧騒、人ごみ、クラクションを鳴らしながら走り抜けるたくさんのバイク。マラケシュのスークは、ラ・マモーニアの静謐さとは対照的だ。
　さらに、街灯にも乏しいメディナ（旧市街）の奥にある、看板も目印もない築200年以上の古い石造りのレストラン、ヤクートでのディナー。いったん中に入ると、そこはアラビアンナイトの別世界が広がる。
　つくづく思った。
　男性読者に方には、心から愛する女性にめぐり逢ったら、ぜひマラケシュに一緒に行くことをお勧めする。女性読者の方には、心から愛する男性がみつかったら、「連れて行って」とぜひお願いしてほしい（もちろん、「私が連れていく」でも「一緒に行こう」でもいいが）。

　I have never visited such an exotic town as Marakech.
　The Noise, the crowd, and motorcycles passing through the croud with horn. The Souq in Marakech is in totally constrast to tranquility in La Mamounia. Furthermore, a dinner at Yacout, an over 200-years-old stonework mansion without any sign nor mark in a deep area of the old town, Medina. Once you enter into the place, it is a different world of the Arabian Nights.
　I heartily thought that you should take your love to Marakech…

ラ・マモーニアの正面玄関。
The main entrance of La Mamounia

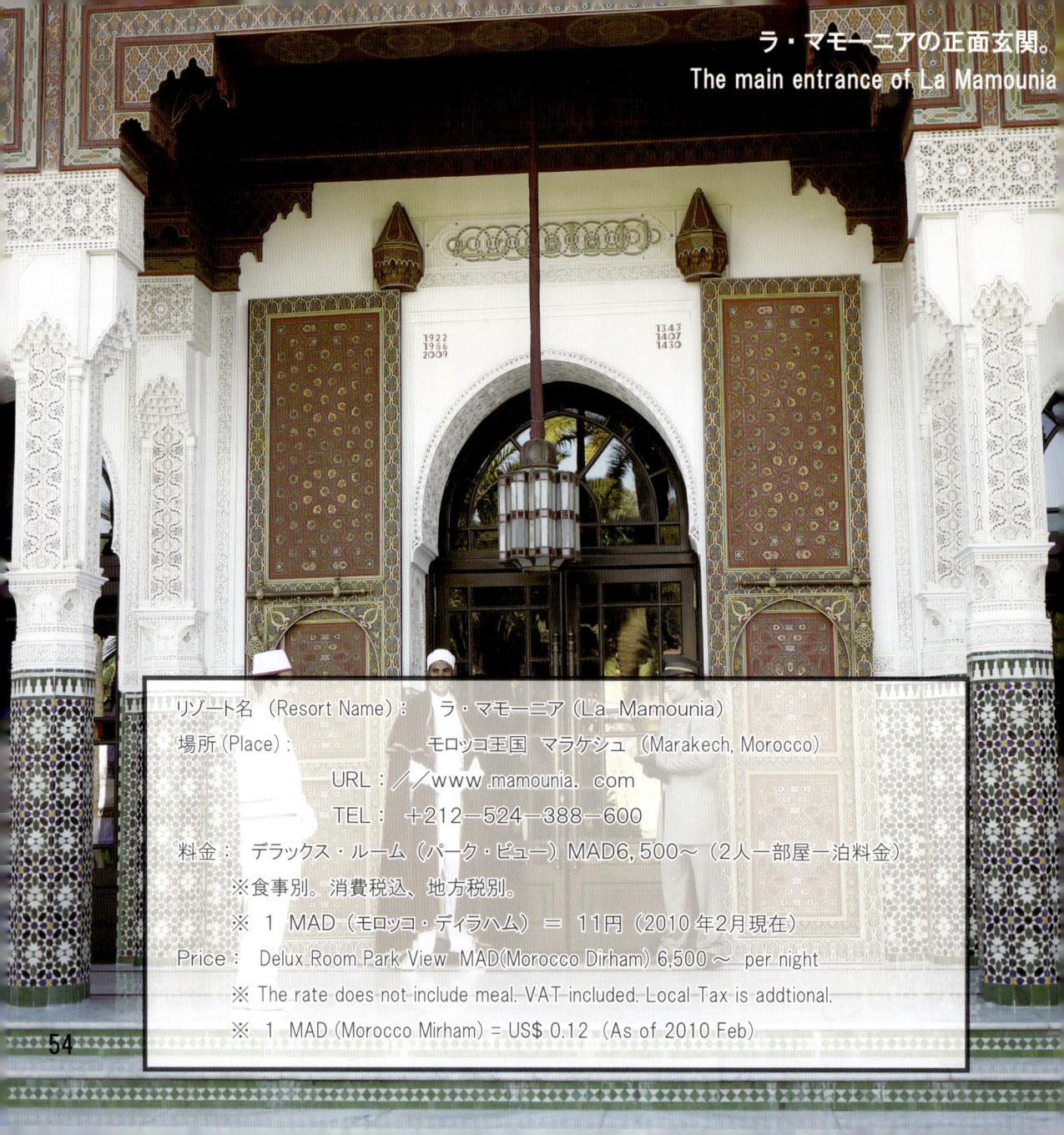

リゾート名（Resort Name）： ラ・マモーニア（La Mamounia）

場所（Place）： モロッコ王国 マラケシュ （Marakech, Morocco）

URL：//www.mamounia.com

TEL： +212-524-388-600

料金： デラックス・ルーム（パーク・ビュー）MAD6,500〜（2人一部屋一泊料金）

※食事別。消費税込、地方税別。

※ 1 MAD（モロッコ・ディラハム）＝ 11円（2010年2月現在）

Price： Delux Room Park View MAD(Morocco Dirham) 6,500〜 per night

※ The rate does not include meal. VAT included. Local Tax is addtional.

※ 1 MAD (Morocco Mirham) = US$ 0.12 (As of 2010 Feb)

2001年の大学入試センター試験・世界史Bで「第二次世界大戦における日本の敗戦処理に関して述べた文として正しいもの」を選ぶ問題が出題され、選択肢の1番として「カイロ会談には中国の代表も参加し、台湾の返還が決定された」という文があった。

In a question of "World History" of a Japanse SAT exam in 2001, "is the following sentence true or false, related to the management of Japan after the World War Two?", and the first sentence was that "the delegate from China also attended to Cairo Conference and there the return of Taiwan was decided."

Mena House Oberoi
Cairo, Egypt

55

Mena House Oberoi

مينا هاوس اوبروي

1869　　　　　　　　　　١٨٦٩

先の写真を見ればわかるとおり、1943年のカイロ会議では、英国のチャーチル首相、米国のルーズベルト大統領、中国の蒋介石の3人会談した。その歴史的な会談の場がこのメナ・ハウス・オベロイだ。つまり、先の問題の答えは「正しい」だ。

As you see in the last photo, Prime Minister Churchill, President Roosevelt, and General Chiang Kai-shek from China attended to Cairo Conference. The historical conference was held at this resort, Mena House Oberoi. That means the answer to the question is "true".

しかし、このホテルの現代的な意義は、「ギザのピラミッドに徒歩3分で行ける」ということだろう。3つのピラミッドとスフィンクスの外観を見るだけで、2時間前後の時間がかかる。足場が砂だから歩きづらく、体力が必要だ。

Apart from such a historical meaning of this resort, nowaday this resort has the important position physically, in terms that "we can visit the Giza Pyramids in 3 minutes on foot from the resort." It takes about 2 hours to look at the outside of three pyramids and the Sphinx. It is not so easy to walk there, because of the sand ground. You need to train yourself to walk for a couples of hours, prior to the visit.

1 ピラミッド側からの部屋の窓からは、ピラミッドが大きく見える。

We can enjoy the view from the window in the room located at Pyramid side in the resort.

2 エジプトと言えばモロヘイヤ・スープ。ホテル内のレストラン「ハーン・イル・ハリーリ」は24時間オープン。

Molokheiya, "Jew's marrow," Soup is famous in Egypt. "Khan El Khalili Restaurant" in the resort serves you for 24 hours a day.

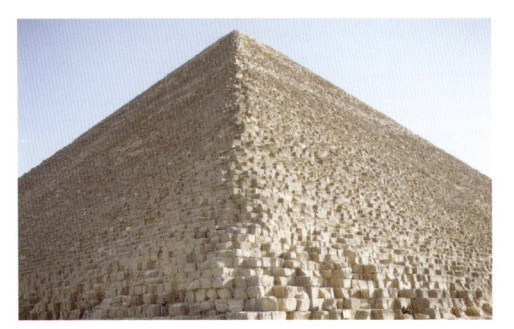

3 ピラミッドは中に入れるが、通路は低く蒸し暑い。大人だと中腰で約80mの狭い上り坂を上る。

We can go into the inside of the Pyramid. The route is so humid and narrow. You have to go up the slope in a half sitting posture.

4 太陽の船博物館がクフ王のピラミッドの裏側にある。何のためのものか不明らしいが、レバノン杉で作られている。

The Khufu Boat Museum is located at the back of Pyramid of King Khufu. The boat is made from Lebanese ceder.

5 レバノン杉は丈夫で腐りにくい。船に最適だ。だから紀元前にフェニキア人は地中海に進出していた。

Lebanese ceder is strong and never decayed. That's the reason why it is used for the boat.

6 スフィンクス側の出口のところにハーン・イル・ハリーリという土産物屋がある。有名なバザールと同じ名前。割引有。

A souvenir shop "Khan El-Khalily", same name as the famous bazar in Cairo, just outside of the Sphinx exit, gives you discount,

7 ギザから車で約30分のカイロ中心部にあるエジプト考古学博物館には必見の「黄金のマスク」がある。

The Egyptian Museum has the famous Mask of Tutankhamun. The museum is located at the center of Cairo, 30 minutes drive from Giza.

8 その博物館はナイル川そばにあり、カイロタワーも見える。老朽化のため新しくギザ地区に日本のODAで建築予定。

The museum is near the Nile River and the Cairo Tower. A new museum is planned to be built at GIza by ODA money from Japan.

59

2階ロビーのシャンデリア
Chandelier on the 2nd floor

予約は必ずピラミッド側の部屋をお勧めする。
できれば、バスルームが大きいスイートが快適だ。
I strongly recommend to make reservation of the room at the Pyramid side. The Delux Suite is comfortable with a large bathroom.

リゾート名（Resort Name）：　メナ・ハウス・オベロイ(Mena House, Oberoi)
場所(Place)：　エジプト・カイロ　(Cairo, Egypt)
URL：／／www.oberoihotels.com
TEL：＋22－2－3377－3222
料金：　デラックス・スイート　760ユーロ〜（2人一部屋一泊料金）※食事別。25％税別。
Price：　Delux Suite Euro760〜　per night ※ w/o meal. 25% tax additional
※パレスウィングは2010年5月からリノベーション。
※ Renovation of Place Wing starting from May 2010.

この写真をみて「どこのラストランだろう？」と思うかもしれない。
You may think that this is a photo of a good restaurant.....

Crockfords Club
London

Ⓒ Crockfords Club

61

ここは世界で最も歴史の古いプライベートカジノクラブだ。マカオの喧騒とは大違い。
This is the world's oldest private Gaming Club. A totally different experience to Noisy Macau.

クラブ名 (Club Name)： クロックフォーズ・クラブ (Crockfords Club)
場所 (Address)： 30 Cruzon St., London, W1JTN, U.K.
URL： //www.crockfords.com
TEL： +44-20-7493-7771
紹介制 (Introduction)：利用には紹介が必要だが、著者までご連絡頂ければ、連絡先をお知らせします。You will need introduction for your first visit. I, the author of this guide, can help you contact the club manager, if you send me an e-mail, guide@ibcg.co.jp 。

62

© Crockfords Club

ここはスポーツ選手やハリウッド・スターというよりも、中東やロシアの裕福なビジネスマンが人目を避けてこっそりとカジノを楽しみに来るところだ。場所もロンドン中心地、メイフェア。外観もシックだ。

Rich international businessmen mainly from the Middle East and Russia, rather than profesional sport players or Hollywood stars, come to this club to enjoy private gaming. This club is in Mayfair, the heart of London. The external appearamce of the building is also very chic.

© Crockfords Club

ICEHOTEL
Sweden

アイスホテルは有名だ。
　あまりに有名だと行く気が失せるのが常だが、刺激中毒の私が、一度はチャレンジしたかったのが、このアイスホテルだ。
　部屋は氷でできていて、ベッドまで氷だ。氷のベッドの上にトナカイの皮を敷いて、冬山登山用の高性能寝袋で寝る。室内はマイナス5度だ。
　本当にそんな環境で寝ることができるのか。それを確かめたかった。
　アイスホテルがあるキルナは、ストックホルムからまっすぐ北上すること飛行機で1時間半。1月上旬に訪問したが、夜明けが午前10時、午後1時すぎには夕暮れが始まる。12月の夏至のころは一日中真っ暗だそうだ。
　いちいち防寒を完璧にしないと外に出れない環境は、宇宙服を着て宇宙遊泳に行く気分だ。

　ICEHOTEL is so famous.
　I usually do not want to go to the place too famous, because I usually lose interest. But ICEHOTEL is an exception. I wanted to challenge to stay there.
　Of course the rooms, even the beds, are made of ice. We put a fur of reindieer on the bed. We sleep in a special sleeping bag for winter climbing.
　I wanted to know if I could really sleep in such a circumstance.
　Kiruna, the city ICEHOTEL is located at, is one hour and a half flight from Stockholm.

65

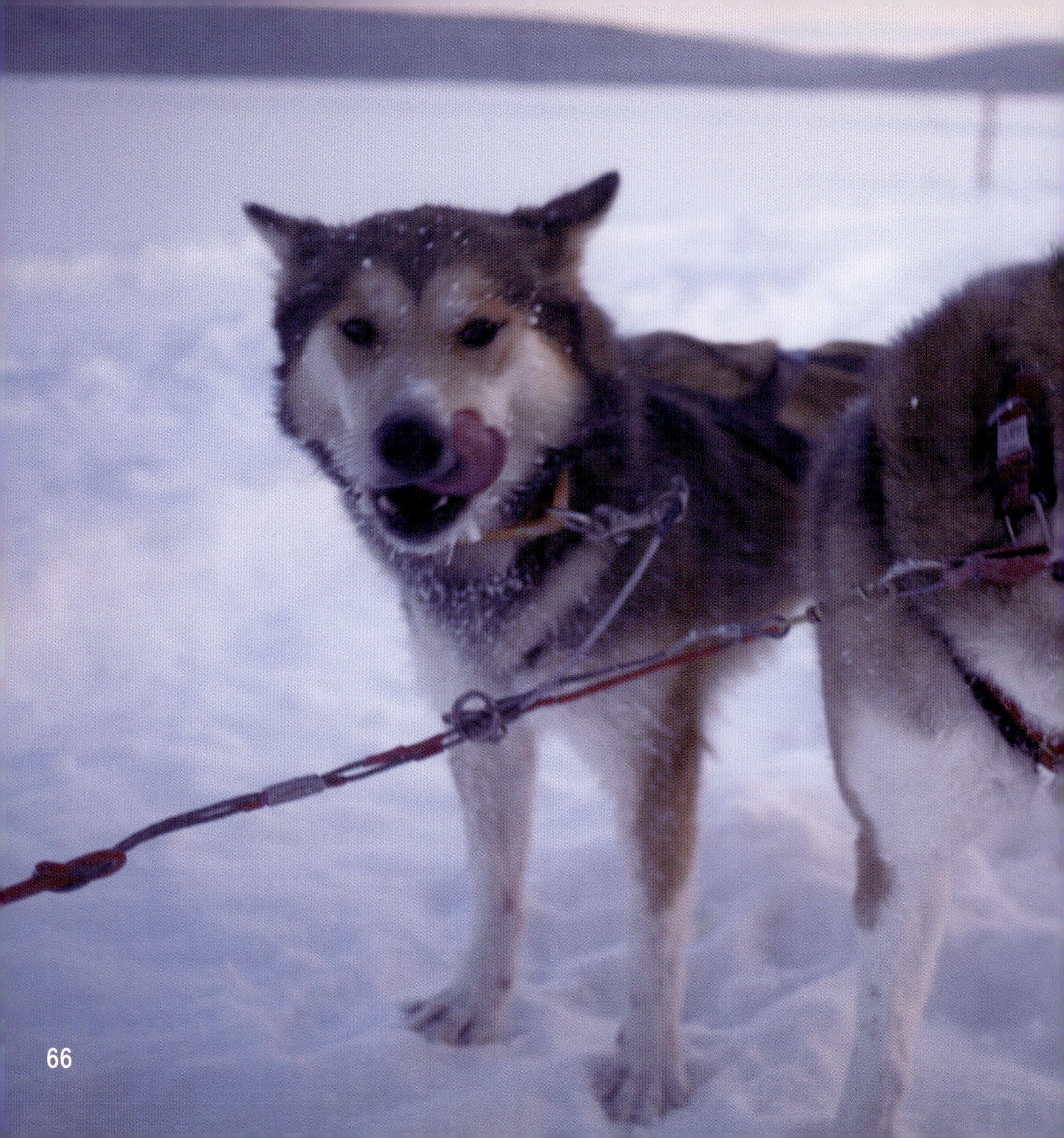

犬ぞりは楽しい。
The dog sledding is fun.

1 事前に予約すると、空港までバスが迎えに来る。空港から15分で到着。降りたとたん、この景色だ。

A bus is waiting for you at the airport, which needs a prior reservation. It takes about 15 minutes from the airport to ICEHOTEL.

2 初日は、いわゆるウォーム・アコモデーションと言われる普通の部屋に泊まった。

On the first night, I stayed at, what is called, "warm accomodation", a normal room. It is warm and comfortable.

3 夜はスノーモービルでオーロラを見に行く「ノーザンライト・ツアー」がお勧め。残念ながら見れなかった。

I recommend you to go to "Northern Lights Tour" at night, where you drive a snowmobile by yourself to see the Northern lights.

4 午前中は犬ぞりだ。想像以上に速い。目だし帽をかぶっていても、冷たい風で顔が凍る。

I recommend you to enjoy dog sledding in the morning, at sunrise time. It is quicker than I expected. My face was frozen by the wind.

5 ランチはブッフェ。真ん中にあるのはトナカイのミートボール。アイスホテルの食事は素材の良さを感じるおいしさだ。

The lunch was buffet. The meat ball in the center of this photo is made from reindeer meat. The food in ICEHOTEL is delicious.

6 ラップ人の村を訪れるアクティビティもある。これがラップ人が生活するテントだ。

There is an activity to learn Sami people's culture. I visited a Sami tent.

レストランと宿泊エリアの間の道路。
The road between the restaurant and the accomodation area.

至るところに樹氷がある。
Foarfrost on trees.

7 ラップの村ではトナカイそりの体験があるが、トナカイは犬がほえないと怠けて進まない（苦笑）。

I experienced the reindeer sledding at the Sami village. As the reindeer is so lazy, the sled can go ahead as long as dogs keep barking.

8 ラップのテントの中で、トナカイの焼き肉をご馳走になる。焚き火の上にフライパンをのせて豪快に焼く。

The Sami person treated us reindeer steakes in the tent. He put a frypan on fire.

9 アイスバーがある。東京にあるのもその支店だ。椅子もテーブルも氷でできている。

The resort has an ICEBAR. It has a branch in Tokyo. The tables and chairs are also made of ice.

10 グラスも氷でできている。ウォッカのカクテルばかりだが、寒いので、飲んでも酔う感じしない。

Even the glass is made of ice. ICEBAR serves vodka cocktails, I could not get drunk because of the cold temperature.

71

昼間でも気温はマイナス10度以下だ。
The temperature was under minus 10 degree Celsius even in dayime.

氷の部屋で寝るときは、手袋と帽子を身につけて寝袋に入る。
You wear a warm cap and mittens, when you sleep in the sleeping bag.

12

アイスルームには荷物を持ち込めない。凍ったり、湿気ったりするからだ。荷物は各部屋ごとにロッカーがあるので、そちらに置く。

You do not bring anything into ICEROOM, because it may be frozen and wet. You leave your luggage in your locker room.

13

僕は氷のベッドでもよく寝れた。朝、起きたら、サウナに直行だ。

I slept well in the ICEROOM. After I got up, I went to Sauna.

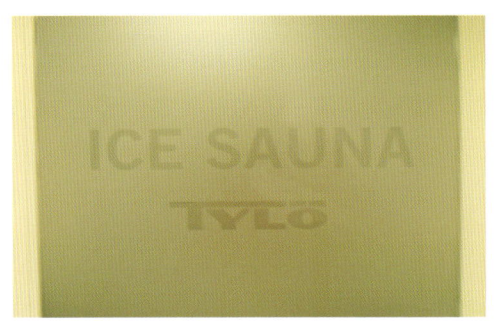

14

サウナの隣に「アイスサウナ」と書いたドアがあった。サウナで身体が熱くなったので、ちょうどよいとドアを開けると…

There was a door of "ICE SAUNA", next to Sauna. "Oh, it is good. Now I got hot by Sauna." I opened the door, then.....

15

そこは屋外だった。実はそこは誰でも通れる通路にもなっていたので、全裸を見られるところだった（苦笑）。

It was outside! The space is a kind of public space so that anybody can pass there. My naked wonderful body came near being seen.

74

アクティビティの集合は、Mのしるしのミーティング・ポイントで。
You gather at this M mark Meeting Point for activities.

ホテル名（Resort Name）：	アイスホテル（ICEHOTEL）
場所(Place)：	スウェーデン、キルナ（Kiruna, Sweden）
	URL：／／www.icehotel.com
	TEL： +46-980-66-800
料金：	アートスイート（1室2名。木〜日）SEK5,800〜
	※朝食・昼食付。
	※1SKR（スウェーデン・クローナ）＝約12.4円（2010年2月現在）
Price:	Art Suite （2 persons. Thu〜Sum）SEK5,800〜
	※ including breakfast and lunch.
	※1SKR＝ about US＄0.14 (as of Feb 2010)

1 アイスホテルのキルナに行くには、ストックホルムで乗り換えが一般的。ノーベル記念館でのみ販売のメダルチョコ。

You may transit at Stockholm on the way to Kiruna. The photo is a Nobel Prize Medal chocolate sold only at Nobel Museum.

2 ダイナマイト型キャンディー。ストックホルムでの宿泊は、ノーベル賞受賞者も宿泊するグランドホテルが最高だ。

This photo is dynamite shaped candy. You should stay at Grand Hotel in Stockholm, which Nobel laureates also stay at. It is great.

3 ストックホルムのディナーは「F12」がおすすめ。テイスティングメニューは小皿で全11品。値段はSEK 1195 だ。

A restaurant "F12" is one of the best restaurants in Stockholm. The Tasting Menu had total 11 dishes, SKR 1195. The chef, ……

4 シェフの感性でつくる。例えば、「サンドイッチとココアを詰めたバックパックをもってでかけたスケート遠足」等だ。

Dnyel Couet, cooks it with sensations like "Long-distance ice-skating with a backpack filled with Sandwiches and hot chocolate".

右下には「Hasta la victoria siempre」という有名な名文句が刻まれる。諸説あるが、「勝利の日まで永遠に」という意味だ。社会主義国だけにワンフレーズのプロパガンダが上手だ。
A famous message of Che " Hasta la victoria siempre", "Until the victory, forever", is written at the lower right.

革命広場のチェ・ゲバラのネオンサイン。
Neon sign of Che Guevara, Plaza de la Revolucion.

いたるところに51周年記念ポスターが貼られていた。

Many posters for the 51st anniversary were put up in Havana.

CUBA

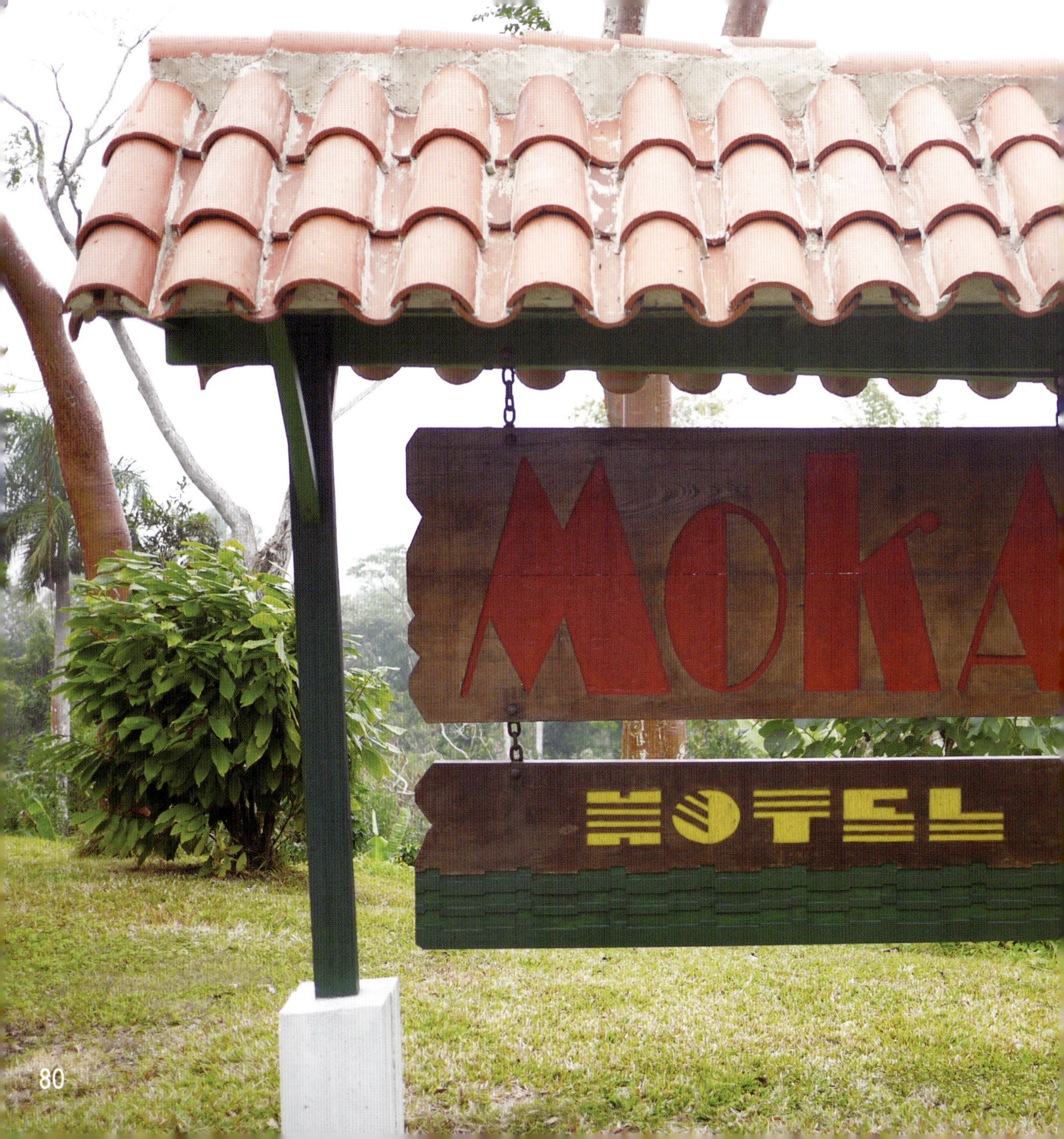
MOKA
HOTEL

キューバは、チェ・ゲバラ、ヘミングウェイ、音楽、踊り、葉巻などが有名だが、今回は「コミュニティ・ホテル」という新しいコンセプトのホテルを訪問した。

　ハバナから車で約一時間西側に行くと、ラス・テラサスという自然保護区がある。19世紀初めにハリケーン被害でハイチから避難してきたフランス人がコーヒー農園を開墾。その後、ブラジルコーヒーの台頭でコーヒーから撤退し、炭生産のために木を伐採。荒廃した土地にキューバ政府は1960年代後半から植林を始めた。1970年以後、森の中で分散して住んでいた人たちを、生活向上のために一か所に集め、コニュニティ（生活共同体）をつくった。その自然保護区に生息する多くの動植物を活用し、外貨獲得のために小さなホテルをつくったのがこの「モカ・ホテル」である。

　Cuba is famous for Che Guevara, Hemingway, Salsa, Cigar and so on. This time I visited a hotel with a new concept, "community hotel".

　One hour drive west from Havana takes us to a bio sphere reserve area called Las Terrazas. The place used to be a coffee farm made by French poeple, who came from Haiti, in early 19th century. From 1960, Cuba government started afforestation and gather people living the area into a one place to improve their life.

　Now the reserve has a small hotel named "Moka Hotel".

1 キューバでは古い車が元気に走っている。このスケルトン状態の車も現役だ。

Old cars still run in Cuba. This skeleton car is also still active.

2 コーヒー豆の乾燥場。下から徐々に乾かし、上の段に上げていく。

The place of this photo is used to be a dry area of coffee beans. Dried beans at lower floor were moved up to the higher floor.

3 一番上では乾いたコーヒー豆を、この大きな機械で細かくする。奴隷の作業だった。

The highest floor has this coffee mill, where slaves from Haiti worked like this.

4 コミュニティには、カフェ・デ・マリアという喫茶店もある。

This community has a coffee shop named "Cafe de Maria."

彼女がマリアさん。お家の隣がお店。ネルドリップの濃いコーヒーを味わえる。
She is Maria. We enjoy a strong coffee filtered through cotton flannel.

Moka Hotel is consisted of a main building with 26 rooms and 3 villas, each of which is an annex to the house of the residents of the community.

モカ・ホテルはメインビルの26室の客室のほか、コミュニティ（集落）の住民の家に併設されたヴィラ3室からなる。写真はコミュニティ。

5 住民の家の台所を通って客室に行く。写真は「大家さん」のバルバリータさんと著者。

You go to your guest room through the kitchen of the resident. The photo shows Barbarita, the resident, and myself in the kichen.

6 ドアより奥は普通の客室だ。ベッドやトイレはもちろん、テレビ、エアコン、バスタブ、屋外シャワーブースもある。

After the door with key, it is a normal guest room with beds, TV, air conditioner, bathroom, bathtub, and even outside shower booth.

7 これがメイン・ビルディング。フロントやレストラン、ショップなどがある。

This is the main building, which has the hotel front, a restaurant, and a shop, with 26 guest rooms.

8 コニュニティには、キューバ唯一の有機野菜レストラン、エル・ロメロがある。雑味のない本当の野菜の味がする。

The community has an eco-restaurant El Romero, the best organic vegetable restaurant in Cuba. The taste is pure.

85

9 お土産屋さんでは、手作りの民芸品がある。1兌換ペソ（1米ドル）から。

We can buy handmade souvenirs from 1 CUC at the souvenir shop.

10 コミュニティ内では、動物は放し飼いだ。朝食の卵料理もおいしい。

They put chickens out to pasture in the community. The egg served as breakfast was also very good.

　コミュニティ・ホテルは民宿とは違う。住民とは挨拶を除くと接点はない。ただ、客室の窓を開けるとコミュニティの生活が見える。生活の音も聞こえる。子どもが遊ぶ声、隣室の住民の夫婦の会話、犬の遠吠え。朝は午前5時に鶏の鳴き声で目が覚める。森の朝特有の湿った新鮮な空気だ。北海道の田舎出身の私は、子どもの頃の夏休みの朝を思い出した。日本を遥か離れたキューバにいて、30年以上前の故郷を思い出し、泣いた。

　A community hotel is different from a guesthouse. We do not have to communicate the residents, apart from greetings. But I saw the normal life of the community from the window of my room. I listened to voices of children playing outside, a conversation of the couple living nextdoor, and howls of dogs. The cluck of chickens woke me up at 5 A.M. The air was humid and fresh, which was peculiar to that of forests in early morning. It recalled an early morning in a summer vacation in my childhood, as I had grown up in Hokkaido, a north area of Japan, very rural. I remembered my country of over 30 years ago and had to cry.

モカという名前は、コーヒーのモカと同じ由来であるが、イエメンの港の名前から取ったとのこと。
The origin of the name "Moka" came from the name of a port in Yemen, same as Mocha coffee.

ホテル名（Resort Name）：	モカ・ホテル（MOKA HOTEL）
場所(Place)：	キューバ、ラス・テラサス（Las Terrazas, Cuba）
URL：	//www.hotelmoka-lasterrazas.com
TEL：	+53-48-578603
料金：	Villa（1室2名）CUC（兌換ペソ）85〜

※朝食付。税・サービスなし。
※1CUC（キューバ兌換ペソ）＝1 US＄＝90円（2010年3月現在）

Price: Villa (2 persons) CUC85〜
※ including breakfast. No tax and no service charge.
※1CUC＝1 US＄ (as of March 2010)

1 ハバナ。ホテル・アンボス・ムンドスに住んでいたヘミングウェイはバー・フロリディータで毎日ダイキリを飲んだという。

I moved to Havana. Ernest Hemingway, who lived at Hotel Ambos Mundos, went to Bar Floridita every day to drink Daiquiri.

2 革命博物館のホセ・マルティの像そばには弾丸の跡。カストロやゲバラが密航に使ったグランマ号の展示もあり。

I found many holes made by bullets, behind Jose Marti's statue at Museo de la Revolucion. It has the Granma, by which Castro entered here.

3 ハバナ市内には40年以上前の古いアメ車やソ連製の車が普通に走っている。日本に持って帰るのは不可能とのこと。

We find many over 40 years old American and CCCP cars anywhere in Havana. It needs a special permission to export them to Japan.

4 現地ペソの3ペソはゲバラの絵柄。近々通貨が変更になるらしい。将来、お宝になること間違いなし！

The note of Local 3 peso has a picture of Che Guevara. In the near future, the currency may change. This note will be very precious later.

88

Photo courtesy of The Carlyle, a Rosewood Hotel.

The Carlyle
New York

Photo courtesy of The Carlyle, a Rosewood Hotel.

ウッディ・アレンのライブは毎週月曜日。カバーチャージは一人 US$ 110だ。人気があるので早めに予約。
You had better make reservation for Woody Allen's performance earlier, as the show is so popular. The cover charge costs US$110 per preson.

ニューヨークは、客先のカリブから東京への乗り継ぎのため、1年に何度も立ち寄る。最近はこの The Carlyle に宿泊することが多い。有名人の人であれば、入口が狭くて1つでプライバシーが守られるから、という理由だろう。僕の場合は、夜、静かであるから。また、何よりも、月曜日の夜であれば、カフェ・カーライルでウッディー・アレンのライブが観れるからだ。夜8時40分スタート。約1時間。擦り切れた襟の清潔な青いボタンダウンシャツ。74歳と高齢のためか、自分がクラリネットを吹かないときは寝ている（苦笑）。とにかく最高だ。おそらく今年（2010年）か来年あたりが見おさめだろう。

　I stop over at New York once a quarter, on the way back to Tokyo from Caribbean islands. I often stay at The Carlyle, because it is very quiet at night and very comfortable. Also because I can enjoy Woody Allen's live performance at Cafe Carlyle on Monday night. It starts from 8:40 P.M. for almost one hour. He weared a clean and blue button-down shirt with worn-out collar. As he is 74 years old, he looked sleepy, when he did not play his clarinet. But anyway his band's performance is the greatest and entertaining. I am afraid that he may quit the live performance soon, because of the old age. You should stay at the Carlyle on Monday night and enjoy the performance at Cafe Carlyle right now.

ホテル名 （Resort Name）：
　　　　ザ・カーライル （The Carlyle）
場所 (Adress)： 米国ニューヨーク
　　　37 East 76th Street, New York, NY
URL：//www.thecarlyle.com
TEL： +1-212-744-1600
料金：クラシック・ルーム　US＄755〜
　　　※朝食別。税14.75％別。

Price: Classic Room　US＄755〜
　　　※ without meals.
　　　※ 14.75% tax additional.

あとがき

思いつくことを若干書く。昨年（2009年）3月に前作「痩せる！チバソム」を出版した。それをご覧になった日経BP社発行の月刊誌「日経TOPLEADER」の編集長から、知られていない海外リゾートを紹介するコラム「世界一ほっとする時間」の連載を依頼された。おかげさまで2年目突入だ。また、私があまりによく世界をうろちょろしていることをご覧になった毎日新聞社発行の月刊誌「エコノミスト・マネー」の編集長からは「金融放浪記」という連載を依頼された。この場を借りて、表現する場を与えていただいた二人の編集長にはお礼を申し上げたい。また、情報は発信してみるものだ、と改めて思った。

今となっては、その2つの連載が自分の日記代わりになっている。この「シワ消える！コモ・シャンバラ」を書くにあたっては、過去に自分が書いたコラムをよく読み返した。

前回のガイドがカリブ中心だったとすれば、今回は比較的アフリカが多い。刺激中毒の私がこの本で紹介するところは、感じ方は人それぞれかもしれないが、何がしかのサプライズがあると思う。万人受けしそうなところで言えば、マラケシュの「ラ・マモーニア」の美しさ、「ワン＆オンリー・ケープタウン」の快適さは「鉄板」だろう。本文でも書いたが、特に「ラ・マモーニア」はぜひ彼女あるいは彼と行くべきだ。

行きやすいところでいけば、タイトルにしたバリの「コモシャンバラ・エステート」は比較的近いから行きやすいし、NYの「ザ・カーライル」も人気のNYだから行きやすいと思う。こう言うと本人に怒られるだろうが、ウッディ・アレンのバンドの演奏は本当に見ていて楽しい。顔の血管が浮き出るほど一生懸命演奏しているが、それでも年のせいか、彼のクラリネットの高音はとぎれがちだった。おじいちゃん、頑張れ！と応援したくなる。圧巻は最後の曲だ。最後はクラリネットを片づけながら、歌を歌うのだが、そのエンターテイナーぶりは見事の一言だ。日本で言えば、高木ブーのライブのように楽しめる。夢の共演があればいいのに、と個人的には思う。本文に書き忘れたが、ザ・カーライルのカフェ・カーライルでは、名物の「ドーバー・ソール」がお勧めだ。ドーバー海峡の舌ヒラメのソテーだが、大きくて肉厚でジューシーだ。

放浪癖が抜けない私は、日本に戻るとすぐに、次はどこに行こうかと考える。南米には足を踏み入れたことがない。オセアニアも手薄だ。砂漠を旅してみたいとも思う。今回はエジプトのピラミッドを訪ねたが、今は閉鎖中のマチュピチュやナスカの地上絵、イースター島などのベタなところは意外と行っていない。仕事のついでに寄ることが多いので、観光だけのところだとなかなか行けない。ご購入ありがとうございました。ご意見・ご感想などは guide@ibcg.co.jp まで、メールをいただけましたら幸いです。石井至

Postscript

This is the 2nd travel guide written by me. The title of first one was "We slim at Chiva-Som ~ famous resorts for global rich celebrities, but unknown in Japan". Chiva-Som is a resort in Thailand, where we can reduce our weight just by eating as much as possible there. The foods are special, produced by a genius chef, Mr. Paisarn Cheewinsiriwat. The first travel guide, published in March 2009, mainly introduced resorts in Caribbean islands. But this 2nd one picks up more from African Continent than from other areas.

After the 1st travel guide was published, I was asked to write a regular column related to resorts outside of Japan, by the editor-in-chief of a monthly magazine "Nikkei Topleader". Now the column goes on and the 2nd year has started. I was asked a different regular column, too, by the editor-in-chief of a monthly magazine "Economist Money" issued by The Mainichi Newspapers. The titile of the column is "Financial Drifter's Diary", the editor-in-chief came to know that I am moving around the world every day, by reading the 1st travel guide.

I used to work for financial institutions and am still now providing consulting services to foreign governments. That's the reason why the title of the 2nd column has a word of "Financial".

Related to this travel guide, one of the most enjoyable time was Woody Allen's live performance at Cafe Carlyle. The dish we should taste there is "Dover Sole", which was so juicy, large, and thick, though I forgot to write it in the text.

Though I am afraid that Woody Allen may be upset to hear the following, high sounds of his clarinet was not so smooth, because, I guess, he is old. I wanted to cheer him on, in listening to his music. But the last song was so nice. He took his clarinet apart and started to sing the song from the middle of the music, with putting the parts of the clarinet back to the case. And his song ended, the moment he closed the lid of the case.

Where should I go next? I've never been to South America and have a limted experience in Oceania. I also would like to cross any desert area by riding a camel.

Anyway, thank you very much for reading this travel guide. If you have any comment, send me an e-mail to: guide@ibcg.co.jp. Your comments are welcome.   Itaru Ishii

日本人のあまり行かない

- ICEHOTEL (P64-)
- Crockfords Club (P61-)
- Mena House, Oberoi (P55-)
- Six Senses Hideaway, Zighy Bay (P11-)
- Capella Singapore (P8-)
- La Mamounia (P41-)
- Singita Sabi Sand, Boulders Lodge (P33-)
- COMO Shambhala Estate Bali, Indonesia (P1-)
- One&Only Cape Town (P23-)
- Hospitality Ticket FIFA World Cup (P29-)

世界のセレブ・リゾート２

目次 CONTENTS

COMO Shambhala Estate	P1
Capella Singappore	P8
Six Senses Hideaway, Zighy Bay	P11
One&Only Cape Town	P23
Hospitality Ticket FIFA World Cup	P29
Singita Sabi Sand, Boulders Lodge	P33
La Mamounia	P41
Mena House, Oberoi	P55
Crockfords Club	P61
ICEHOTEL	P64
Moka Hotel	P78
The Carlyle	P89
あとがき	P92
Postscript	P93

※この本に書かれている内容は、事前のお知らせなく変更されている場合があります。また、ホテル等からの情報提供に基づき、あるいは、独自に調べた上で記載しておりますが、内容が事実と異なる場合もあり得ますので、ご了承下さい。

著者紹介

石井 至 1965年、北海道手稲町（現・札幌市手稲区）生まれ。東京大学医学部卒。東京大学大学院医学系研究科修士課程修了（修士号）。米・スイス・仏系銀行でデリバティブ商品開発などに従事。28歳でマネージング・ディレクター就任は日本人最年少記録。32歳で引退後、石井兄弟社設立。現在、当社取締役社長。著書は、前作『痩せる！チバソム』（当社刊）ほか多数。

シワ消える！ コモ・シャンバラ
日本人のあまり行かない世界のセレブ・リゾート 2

2010年4月5日　初版第1刷発行

　　　　　著者　石井 至
　　　　発行人　石井 至
　　発行・販売　石井兄弟社
　　　　　　　〒150-0001
　　　　　　　東京都渋谷区神宮前1-17-5-503
　　　　　　　電話：03-5775-1385／FAX：03-5775-1386

　　印刷・製本　株式会社シナノ

ISBN 978-4-903852-04-1

Printed in Japan

Copyright © 2010 Itaru Ishii. All right reserved

落丁・乱丁本はお取り替えいたします。